I CAN WRITE A BOOK REPORT

by
Patricia Carratello

Illustrated by
Rick Chacón

Teacher Created Materials, Inc.
P. O. Box 1214
Huntington Beach, CA 92649
© Teacher Created Materials 1985
ISBN 1-55734-336-5

Teacher Created Materials

To the Teacher:

I Can Write A Book Report provides your students with information on how to make reports on non-fiction and fiction books.

The book begins by encouraging the students to read, read, read! Then explanations are given of non-fiction and fiction books.

The remaining pages of the book contain specific book report ideas, first for non-fiction, then for fiction. These are lessons for many creative and enjoyable ways to present book reports.

We hope your students and you enjoy these ideas. They will add a new interest and enthusiasm to the book-reporting process, for your students *and* you!

TABLE OF CONTENTS

WHY READ?

Reading is interesting and fun!

You can read books to learn many things. It is interesting to read and find out things you don't know. Reading helps your **knowledge** grow!

FILL IN THE BLANKS BELOW.

These are some things I would like to learn more about:

1. animal: _____

2. sport: _____

3. hobby: _____

4. person: _____

5. time in history: _____

You can also read books for enjoyment. It is fun to read and "become" the person you are reading about, or "travel" to another time and place. Reading helps your **imagination** grow!

FILL IN THE BLANKS BELOW.

These are some things I would like to imagine:

1. person or creature (describe!) _____

_____

2. time (describe!)_____

_____

3. place (describe!) _____

_____

It is important to become a good reader. Reading is a skill you will use for your entire life. You will read in school, at home, and in play. You **need** to **read**!

WRITE THE NAME OF THE BEST BOOK YOU HAVE EVER READ.

_____

WRITE THE NAME OF A BOOK YOU WOULD LIKE TO READ.

_____

Go to the **library** and get it! Reading is **interesting** and **fun**!

TYPES OF BOOKS

There are two types of books you will learn about on this page. One type is fiction and the other type is non-fiction.

Fiction books are books that are **made-up.** They are stories that authors have imagined. A fiction book could be about a friendship between a boy and a horse, a mystery of a lost treasure, or an adventure in a ship sailing the sea. When you read a fiction book, you really use your **imagination!**

Non-fiction books are books that are **true.** They contain many facts about things. A non-fiction book could be about the history of a country, the life of a person, or facts about an animal. When you read a non-fiction book, you really find out a lot of interesting **facts!**

> Can you tell which books are **fiction** and which are **non-fiction** just by the titles? Put each title in the correct column. Be sure to underline the title of each book and use capital letters correctly.

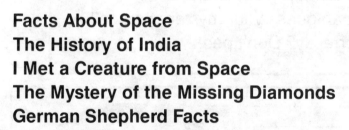

Facts About Space
The History of India
I Met a Creature from Space
The Mystery of the Missing Diamonds
German Shepherd Facts

My Best Friend, My Horse
The Brain - How It Works
The Life of Thomas Edison
The South Sea Adventure
The Lost Treasure on Mystery Island

FICTION (made-up)

1. _____

2. _____

3. _____

4. _____

5. _____

NON-FICTION (true)

1. _____

2. _____

3. _____

4. _____

5. _____

BIOGRAPHY
WHO AM I?

A biography is a book written about the life of a person. It is a **TRUE** story, based on **FACTS.** A biography is **non-fiction.**

Many biographies have been written about the lives of famous people. Some of these people are presidents, explorers, scientists, writers, inventors, artists, and athletes.

Go to the library. Look at the books in the biography section. Choose a biography about a person who seems interesting to you. Read it! Then write one paragraph about what your famous person did to make him or her famous, **BUT, do not** write his or her name in the paragraph! Write the name of the mystery person inside the big question mark. Then cut this paper on the solid lines and fold it on the broken line. Exchange your mystery paragraph with your classmates. How many classmates can guess your mystery person? How many people can you guess correctly? Don't peek!

Who am I?

Who am I?

BIOGRAPHY
TEN QUESTIONS

A biography is a book written about the life of a person. It is a **TRUE** story, based on **FACTS.** A biography is **non-fiction.**

> Go to the library. Look at the books in the biography section. Choose a biography about a person who seems interesting to you. Read it! Then prepare for the game of Ten Questions.

Directions for Ten Questions:
You will now be quizzed about your biographical person by your classmates. They will ask you **one** question at a time. Answer each question the best you can. Your classmates may only ask you ten questions. Then they must try to guess your famous person!

> Prepare for the game now. What are five questions you might be asked about your person? A few questions are given for you to answer. Then think of three more questions you might be asked. Be sure to answer your own questions!

1. Is your famous person male or female? _____

2. In what country did or does your famous person live and work? _____
   _____

3. Question: _____
   _____
   Answer: _____
   _____

4. Question: _____
   _____
   Answer: _____
   _____

5. Question: _____
   _____
   Answer: _____
   _____

INVENTORS AND THEIR INVENTIONS

You read non-fiction books to find out facts about many things. For this assignment, you will read to find out facts about inventors and their inventions.

Choose an inventor or an invention that is interesting to you. Use the encyclopedia and any non-fiction book on the person or subject to answer the questions in the light bulb. (There are inventors and inventions listed outside the light bulb to help you get started.)

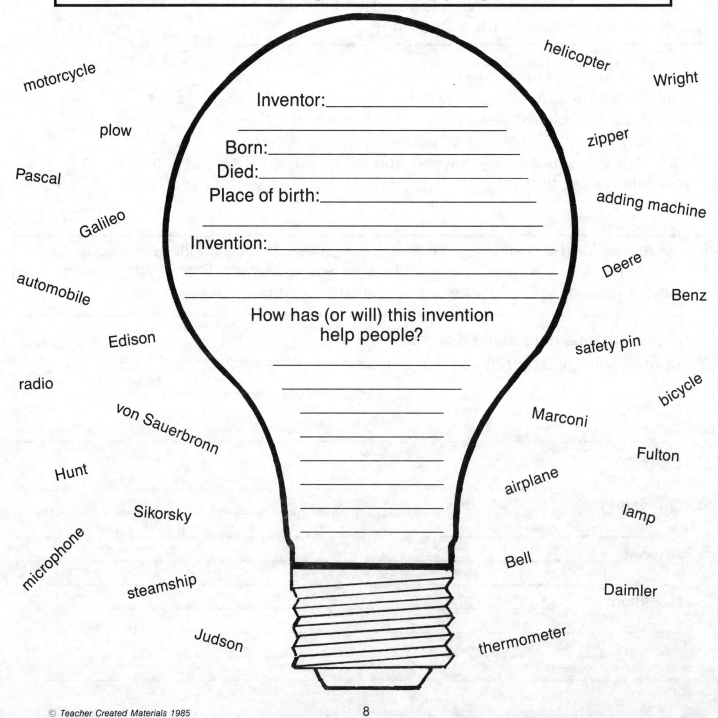

motorcycle

plow

Pascal

Galileo

automobile

Edison

radio

von Sauerbronn

Hunt

Sikorsky

microphone

steamship

Judson

helicopter

Wright

zipper

adding machine

Deere

Benz

safety pin

bicycle

Marconi

Fulton

airplane

lamp

Bell

Daimler

thermometer

Inventor:_____

_____

Born:_____

Died:_____

Place of birth:_____

_____

Invention:_____

_____

_____

How has (or will) this invention help people?

COUNTRY, STATE, OR PROVINCE

You read non-fiction books to find out facts about many things. For this assignment, you will read to find out facts about a country, state, or province.

Choose a country, state, or province that is interesting to you. Look it up in a world atlas and an encyclopedia. Use the atlas to help you draw its shape on this paper. Try to fill up the page with the shape! Then use the encyclopedia or other non-fiction books to answer the questions about your subject below. Keep the questions and your answers **inside** the shape you draw!

Subject: _____

How it got its name: _____

_____

How it was discovered: _____

_____

Population: _____

Three interesting facts:

1. _____

_____

2. _____

_____

3. _____

_____

TIME IN HISTORY — DIORAMA

You read non-fiction books to find out facts about many things. For this assignment, you will read to find out facts about a time in history.

> Choose a time in history you would like to learn more about. It could be the building of the Great Wall in China, the Gold Rush in California, or the first airplane flight! Read about it! Then, follow the directions below to make a diorama of the event.

Title of book: _____

Author: _____ Number of pages: _____

Directions for Diorama

You will need:

1 shoe box	scissors	pen
construction paper	paste	crayons
drawing paper	paint and paint brush	

1. Cover the outside of the shoe box with construction paper.
2. Stand the shoe box on its side and paint the background you want on the inside. Paint ground, sky, mountains, oceans, or whatever else you need.
3. Draw and color the things you need to put inside the box. You may need people, airplanes, trees, tables, or animals, to name a few.
4. Before you cut out the figures, draw a "pasting tab" on the top or bottom of each figure. See diagram.

5. Cut out the figures with the pasting tabs. Fold the tabs over. Put paste on the tabs and place the figures inside the diorama.
6. Fill in the blanks on this diorama label. Cut it out and paste it to the outside top of your diorama.

Diorama Label

Diorama

What?_____

_____

Where? _____

When? _____

By _____ Date_____

TWO SOURCES, ONE SUBJECT

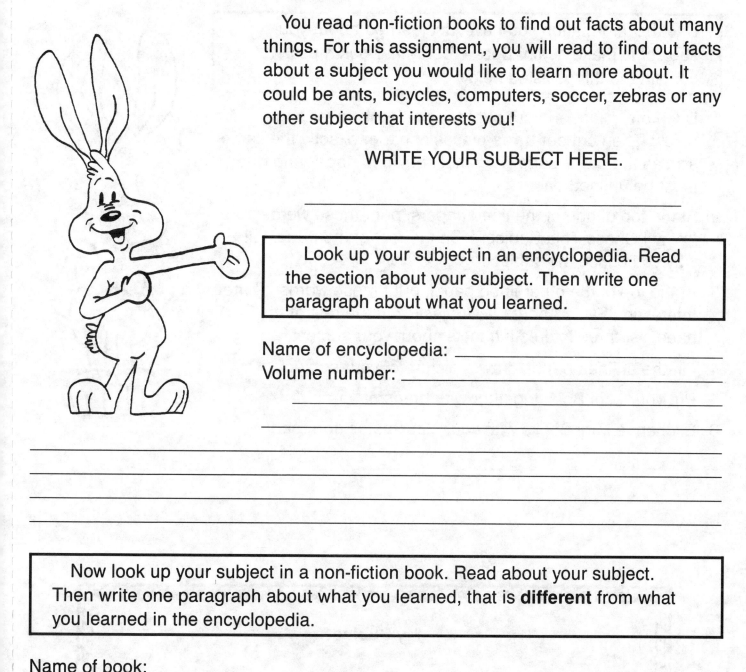

You read non-fiction books to find out facts about many things. For this assignment, you will read to find out facts about a subject you would like to learn more about. It could be ants, bicycles, computers, soccer, zebras or any other subject that interests you!

WRITE YOUR SUBJECT HERE.

_____

Look up your subject in an encyclopedia. Read the section about your subject. Then write one paragraph about what you learned.

Name of encyclopedia: _____

Volume number: _____

_____

_____

_____

_____

_____

Now look up your subject in a non-fiction book. Read about your subject. Then write one paragraph about what you learned, that is **different** from what you learned in the encyclopedia.

Name of book: _____

Author: _____

_____

_____

_____

_____

_____

_____

You will find that an encyclopedia is great if you want to just be "introduced" to a subject. But if you really want to "know" your subject, you need to read about it in a non-fiction book!

MINI BOOK

Use the information you have just learned about your subject to make a Mini Book. Your Mini Book must contain the things listed below.

1. Decorate, fill in, and cut out the Mini Book cover page below. Then cut out **three** pieces of paper exactly the same size as the cover page. **Two** must be lined paper and **one** must be unlined paper.

2. At the top of one of the lined papers, print these words: "Why I Chose This Subject". On the rest of the page, tell why you chose the subject.

3. At the top of the other lined paper, print these words: "Three Interesting Facts About My Subject". On the rest of the page, list three interesting facts about your subject.

4. On the unlined paper, draw a picture of your subject.

5. Put your Mini Book together with brads or yarn.

6. Exchange Mini Books with your classmates and read!

My Subject

_____

by

_____

date

_____

"HOW TO" . . . —
A DEMONSTRATION SPEECH

You read non-fiction books to find out facts about many things. For this assignment, you will read to find out how to do or make something!

> Choose a book that explains how to do or make something. It could be a book about how to play basketball or how to make paper airplanes. Read your book. Now, prepare yourself to give a speech to demonstrate what you learned how to do or make. Give your speech to the class.

Speech Topic: How to _____

_____.

Book: _____

Author: _____

Materials I need to bring for my demonstration speech:

_____

_____

Speech outline (Use this to help you organize your speech.)

In my speech I will show you how to _____

_____.

The first thing is _____

_____.

The second thing is _____

_____.

Next _____

_____.

Then _____

_____.

Finally _____

_____.

I hope my speech has helped you learn how to _____

_____.

POETRY BOOK REPORT

Go to the poetry section of your school or city library. Choose one book of poetry that looks interesting to you. Then answer these questions about your book.

Title of book: _____

_____

Author or editor: _____

Number of pages: _____

Write the titles and authors of five poems you read. (Write the first lines if no titles are given.)

Title	**Author**
1. _____	_____
2. _____	_____
3. _____	_____
4. _____	_____
5. _____	_____

Copy the poem you like the best. Be sure to write the title and author.

Title	**Author**
_____	_____

_____

_____

_____

_____

_____

_____

_____

_____

Why do you like this poem? _____

_____ .

What does it mean to you? _____

_____ .

Now read this poem to the class. Tell your classmates what this poem means to you.

BOOK MARKERS

You read fiction books for enjoyment. It is fun to read and "become" the person you are reading about or "travel" to another time and place!

Mark your place in your books with these special book markers!
Fill in your name, color the markers, then cut them out.
Then **READ!**

loves
to
read!

I'm a
FANTASTIC
reader!

is
reading
this
book!

A SCENE FROM MY STORY

You read fiction books for enjoyment. Sometimes you can make book reports for enjoyment! There are many fun ways to make reports on fiction books. Here is one!

> Choose a part from the fiction book you have just finished. It should be a scene that would be easy for you to memorize. Present the scene from your story to the class. Have fun!

Title of book: _____

_____

Author: _____

Number of pages: _____ Page/pages my scene is on: _____

Who I will be: _____

_____

What I will wear: _____

_____

What I will do: _____

_____

_____

_____

_____

What I will say: _____

_____

_____

_____

_____

_____

_____

_____

_____

_____

"BOOK REPORT"

Directions for making "Book" report found on page 18.

1. Write the title and author of your book on the front cover and the book spine where marked.

2. On the front cover, draw a picture of something from your book. It may be a character or a favorite scene.

3. Write the number of pages in your book on the back cover where marked.

4. Write a one paragraph plot summary (what happened in your book) on the back cover. Practice writing your paragraph on the lines below before you write it on your book.

_____

_____

_____

_____

_____

_____

_____

5. Cut out your "Book" along the outside lines.

6. Fold "flap" pieces at broken lines. Fold spine at broken lines. (Fold the book front flaps like the book back flaps.)

7. Hold paper in one hand and form into a book shape. Paste lined front flaps over unlined back flaps.

8. Share your finished book with other classmates! You might want to join some books together with string to form a mobile!

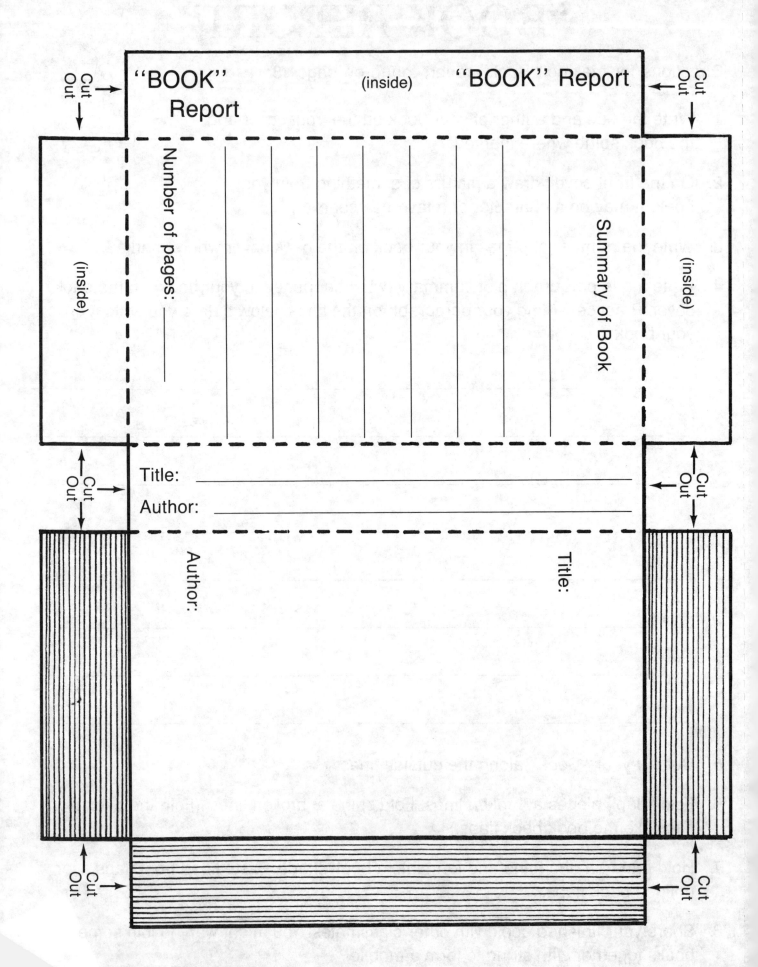

"BOOK" Report

(inside)

"BOOK" Report

Cut Out

Cut Out

(inside)

Number of pages: _____

Summary of Book

(inside)

Cut Out

Cut Out

Title: _____

Author: _____

Author:

Title:

Cut Out

Cut Out

TIME CAPSULE

You are making a time capsule to be buried this week in your city park. The time capsule will be dug up in 100 years. It will show people in the future what was important to you today.

Choose the best book you have ever read. Tell people in the future why it is such a great book. Explain why they should read it, too! Then color your capsule and cut it out. Put it in a box with the time capsules of your classmates. Your teacher will "bury" the box. Once a week, your teacher will "dig it up" and read you a few time capsules. How many of the great books have you read?

Name of book:_____

_____

Author: _____

_____

This is a great book because_____

_____

_____

_____

All the people of the future should read

this book because: _____

_____

_____

_____

_____

19 © Teacher Created Materials 1985

A LETTER TO THE AUTHOR

You have just finished reading _____
_____ by _____.
Write a letter to the author. Tell the author what you liked about the book. If there was anything you didn't like, tell the author about that too! Then think of one question you have about the book. Maybe the author did not tell about what happened to a character and you would really like to know!

_____ your
                                    address

_____ today's date

Dear _____,   name of
                                     author

_____ I

_____ liked . . .

_____

_____

_____

_____ I didn't

_____ like . . .

_____ (or more

_____ I liked . . .)

_____

_____ One

_____ question

_____ I have . . .

        Sincerely,

_____ your name

A CHARACTER COMES TO LIFE!

The main character in your book has just walked into your room at home. Do you know your character well enough to answer these questions? Give COMPLETE answers.

Name of book: _____

_____

Author_____

Main Character_____

Questions: *The following are questions you are asking the main character in the book you just read.*

1. Did you enjoy the book you were in? _____
_____

2. Did you have a favorite character? _____
_____

3. Did you like the ending?_____
_____

4. I have a few questions about some things in the book. Would you give me your answer?

Question #1 _____
_____

Answer #1 _____
_____

Question #2 _____

Answer #2 _____
_____

Question #3 _____

Answer #3 _____
_____

SALES TALK

You are trying to sell the book you have just read. You would like everyone you know to buy it for a birthday present for someone they know. How would you "sell" your classmates the book? How could you make them want to buy it? Fill in the blanks below, then write your sales pitch. When you have practiced what you wrote, present your sales talk to the class!

Title of book: _____

Author: _____ Pages:_____

Price of book: _____ (You can make it up!)

Why everyone should read this book: _____
_____
_____

The most exciting part of the book (Don't give away the ending!): _____
_____
_____

Why this book will make a great gift: _____
_____
_____

My sales talk:

I think everyone in this room should buy at least one copy of this book! Everyone should read this book because _____
_____
_____
_____
_____

The most exciting part of the book was _____
_____
_____
_____
_____

This book will make a great gift because _____
_____
_____

Buy it today! It is only $_____. You couldn't buy a better gift!

COMING ATTRACTION!

Your book is going to be made into a movie! Make a "Coming Attraction" poster for the theater. Fill in the blanks below starting with the title of the book. Then list the main characters and draw a picture of one scene in the book. Finally, write a short paragraph explaining why everyone MUST see the movie! When you have finished your "Coming Attraction" poster, cut it out and display it with other posters made by your classmates. Which "movies" would you want to see?

Starring

You MUST see this movie because _____

PART II!

You have been chosen to write a Part II (sequel) of the book you have just finished reading. Fill in the blanks below. Then write a paragraph telling us what will happen in your new book!

Title of book you read: _____
_____

Author: _____
Pages: _____
Title of new book you will write: _____
_____

Main character: _____
Description of main character:_____
_____

Was this main character in Part I? _____ If so, has he or she changed? _____
Explain: _____
_____
_____

What are some things that are the same in each book? _____
_____
_____
_____

What are some things that are different in each book? _____
_____
_____
_____

This is what will happen in my new book:
_____
_____
_____
_____
_____
_____
_____
_____

Signed,

_____Author

- FORM -
STANDARD FICTION

> Answer the questions on this page about the fiction book you just read.

Title of book: _____

Author: _____ Number of pages:_____

Plot: Write one paragraph about what happened in your story.

_____

_____

_____

_____

_____

_____

Main character: What does your main character look like? _____

_____

_____

What does your main character act like? _____

_____

_____

Setting: Where does your story take place? _____

_____

When does your story take place? _____

_____

Theme: Why do you think the author wrote this story? Was he or she trying to show us something about life? Was the author writing a story to entertain us? Did you learn anything? Why do you think the author wrote the book?

_____

_____

Evaluation: Did you like this book? _____ Why or why not?_____

_____

_____

_____

_____

- FORM -
MYSTERY

There are many kinds of fiction books. One type of fiction book is called a mystery. A mystery story is a story with a **secret** in it. The secret stays hidden just long enough to make you really want to keep reading the book. Gradually, you discover the answer to who did a crime or where a treasure is hidden. Mystery stories have secrets that are fun to discover!

> Answer the questions on this page about the mystery book you just read.

Title of book: _____

Author: _____ Number of pages:_____

Describe the mystery in the book. _____

_____

_____

_____

_____

Who solved the mystery? _____

_____

How was it solved? _____

_____

_____

_____

What do you think might have happened in your story if the mystery had not been solved?_____

_____

_____

_____

_____

- FORM -
ADVENTURE

There are many kinds of fiction books. One type of fiction book is called an adventure.

An adventure story is full of **action.** A lot of exciting things happen in an adventure story and the things usually happen to a brave, daring hero.

> Answer the questions on this page about the adventure book you just read.

Title of book: _____

Author: _____ Number of pages:_____

What was the adventure in the book? _____

_____

_____

_____

Where was the adventure? _____

_____

When was the adventure? _____

_____

Who went on the adventure? _____

_____

What do you think was the most exciting thing that happened in the book? _____

_____

_____

_____

Would you have liked to go on the adventure? _____ Why or why not?

_____

_____

_____

_____

- FORM -
ANIMAL STORY

There are many kinds of fiction books. One type of fiction book is called an animal story.

An animal story is a story with animals in it. The animals are characters in the story and things happen to them. Many animal books also have humans in them. The story then can show the love that can happen between an animal and a human!

> Answer the questions on this page about the animal book you have just read.

Title of book: _____

_____

Author: _____ Number of pages:_____

Describe the animal(s) in the story. (Choose the main animal.)

What type of animal was in the story? _____

_____

What was the animal's name?_____

What did the animal look like?_____

What did the animal act like? _____

_____

What happened to the animal in the book? _____

_____

_____

_____

Were there any humans in the story? _____ Describe how the animal(s) and the human(s) acted toward each other. _____

_____

_____

Would you like to have this animal as a pet? _____ Why or why not?

_____

_____

- FORM -
SCIENCE FICTION OR FANTASY

There are many kinds of fiction books. Two types of fiction books are called science fiction and fantasy.

A science fiction book is a book that describes adventures in places like outer space, other planets and the future.

A fantasy story is a book about things and people that could not be in real life. A fantasy story may sound like it is true, but it could never really happen.

Science fiction and fantasy books both **really** make you use your imagination!

> Answer the questions on this page about the science fiction or fantasy book you have just read.

Title of book:_____

_____

Author: _____ Number of pages:_____

Was this book science fiction or fantasy? _____

Write one paragraph about what happened in the book.

_____

_____

_____

_____

_____

What is in the story that makes it science fiction or fantasy? (Read the definitions at the top of this page.)

_____

_____

_____

_____

Did this book seem real to you? _____ Why or why not? _____

_____

_____

On another paper, draw a character or scene from this book. Attach it to this report!

- FORM -
HISTORICAL FICTION

There are many kinds of fiction books. One type of fiction book is called historical fiction.

Historical fiction books are books about times in our history and stories in those times. The times are real, but the stories are partly made-up or completely made-up. The people in the book may have been real, but the author used his or her imagination to add more to the story!

> Answer the questions on this page about the historical fiction book you have just read.

Title of book: _____

_____

Author: _____ Number of pages:_____

What time in history does this story take place?

_____

Where does this story take place? _____

_____

Are there any characters in your story who are or were real people or animals? _____
If so, who? _____

_____

Who is your favorite character in the story? _____
Describe one thing that he or she says or does that shows us something about this time in history._____

_____

_____

_____

If you could, would you like to live in this time in history? _____ Why or why not? _____

_____

_____

_____

BOOK WHEEL

Color and cut out the Book Wheel and pointer. Use a brad to attach the pointer to the center of the Book Wheel at the dot. Spin the pointer! **Read** a book from the section the arrow points to. Write the name of the book in the section, then spin again! Read again! If your pointer lands on a section you have already filled, spin again! Be sure to read **at least** one book from each section.

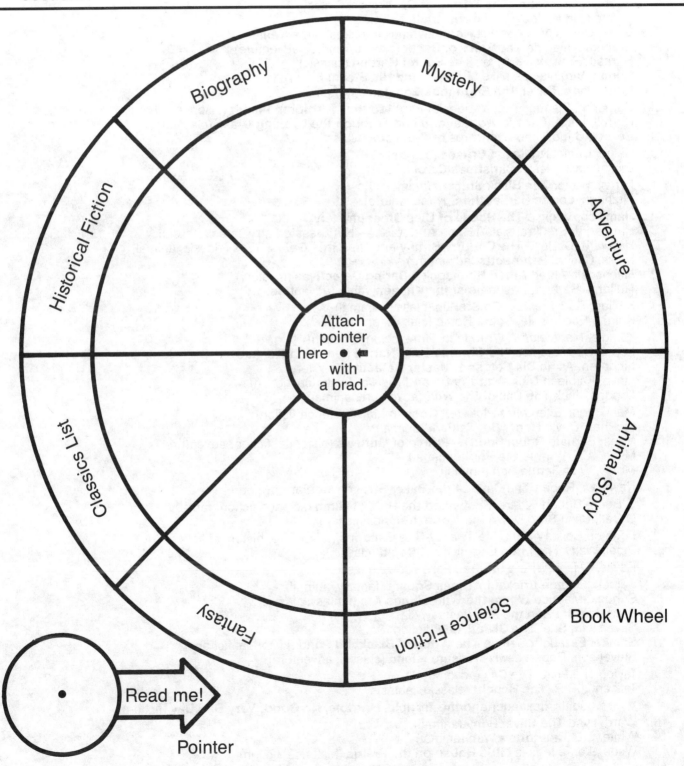

Biography

Mystery

Historical Fiction

Adventure

Attach pointer here ● ⬅ with a brad.

Classics List

Animal Story

Fantasy

Science Fiction

Book Wheel

Read me!

Pointer

BOOK LIST

Here is a book list to help you select a book. Remember, this is only a very **tiny** list. There are many, many more books you will enjoy!

PUT A CHECK MARK NEXT TO EACH BOOK ON THE LIST YOU HAVE READ.

- ☐ Aesop, **Aesop's Fables** (classic)
- ☐ Alcott, Louisa May **Little Women** (classic)
- ☐ Asimov, Isaac **The Best New Thing** (science fiction)
- ☐ Bailey, Carolyn Sherwin **Miss Hickory** (fantasy)
- ☐ Barrie, Sir James **Peter Pan** (classic, fantasy)
- ☐ Baum, Lyman Frank **The Wizard of Oz** (classic, fantasy)
- ☐ Blume, Judy **Tales of a Fourth Grade Nothing** (fiction)
- ☐ Brink, Carol Ryrie **Caddie Woodlawn** (historical fiction, adventure)
- ☐ Brunhoff, Jean de **The Story of Babar** (classic, animal, adventure)
- ☐ Burnett, Frances Hodgson **The Secret Garden** (classic)
- ☐ Burton, Virginia Lee **Mike Mulligan and His Steam Shovel** (classic)
- ☐ Butterworth, Oliver **The Enormous Egg** (fantasy, animal)
- ☐ Cameron, Eleanor **The Wonderful Flight to the Mushroom Planet** (science fiction)
- ☐ Carroll, Lewis **Alice in Wonderland and Through the Looking Glass** (classic)
- ☐ Collodi, Carlo **The Adventures of Pinocchio** (classic)
- ☐ Defoe, Daniel **Robinson Crusoe** (classic)
- ☐ Dickens, Charles **A Christmas Carol** (classic)
- ☐ Farley, Walter **The Black Stallion** (animal)
- ☐ Fitzhugh, Louise **Harriet the Spy** (adventure)
- ☐ Hamilton, Virginia **The House of Dies Drear** (mystery)
- ☐ Haugaard, Erik (translator) **Hans Andersen — His Classic Fairy Tales** (classic)
- ☐ Heyward, DuBose **The Country Bunny and the Little Gold Shoes** (classic, animal)
- ☐ Hicks, Clifford **Peter Potts** (adventure)
- ☐ Hitchcock, Alfred **Alfred Hitchcock's Daring Detectives** (mystery)
- ☐ Holland, Barbara **Prisoners at the Kitchen Table** (adventure)
- ☐ Kipling, Rudyard **Just So Stories** (classic, animal)
- ☐ Knight, Eric **Lassie, Come Home** (classic, animal)
- ☐ L'Engle, Madeleine **A Wrinkle in Time** (science fiction)
- ☐ Lewis, Clive Staples **The Chronicles of Narnia** (fantasy, adventure)
- ☐ Lindgren, Astrid **Bill Bergson, Master Detective** (mystery)
- ☐ Lines, Kathleen **Dick Whittington and His Cat** (historical fiction)
- ☐ London, Jack **The Call of the Wild** (adventure, animal)
- ☐ MacGregor, Ellen **Miss Pickerell Goes to Mars** (science fiction)
- ☐ McPhail, David **Henry Bear's Park** (animal)
- ☐ Miles, Bernard **Robin Hood — Prince of Outlaws** (historical fiction, adventure)
- ☐ Milne, A.A. **Winnie-the-Pooh** (animal)
- ☐ Morey, Walt **Gentle Ben** (animal)
- ☐ Newman, Robert **The Case of the Baker Street Irregular** (mystery)
- ☐ O'Brien, Robert C. **Mrs. Frisby and the Rats of Nimh** (science fiction, fantasy)
- ☐ O'Dell, Scott **Sing Down the Moon** (historical fiction)
- ☐ Pene du Bois, William **The Twenty-One Balloons** (adventure, historical fiction)
- ☐ Piper, Watty **The Little Engine That Could** (classic)
- ☐ Rawls, Wilson **Where the Red Fern Grows** (classic)
- ☐ Selden, George **Cricket in Times Square** (fantasy, animal)
- ☐ Sendak, Maurice **Where the Wild Things Are** (fantasy, classic)
- ☐ Seuss, Dr. **If I Ran the Zoo** (fantasy, classic)
- ☐ Silverstein, Shel **The Giving Tree** (fiction)
- ☐ Speare, Elizabeth George **The Witch of Blackbird Pond** (historical fiction)
- ☐ Stevenson, Robert Lewis **Treasure Island** (classic, adventure)
- ☐ Taylor, Theodore **The Cay** (adventure)
- ☐ Tolkien, J.R.R. **The Hobbitt** (classic, fantasy)
- ☐ Viorst, Judith **Alexander and the Terrible, Horrible, No Good, Very Bad Day** (fiction)
- ☐ Ward, Lynd **The Silver Pony** (animal)
- ☐ White, E.B. **Charlotte's Web** (animal)
- ☐ Wilder, Laura Ingalls **Little House on the Prairie** (historical fiction)